We bring you
everything,
and tip it out
in front of you

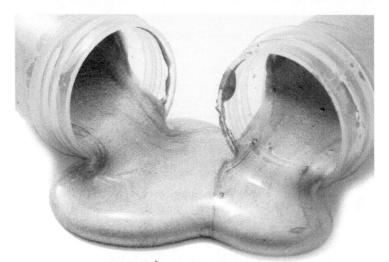

We bring you everything, and tip it out in front of you

New prayers from the Iona Community

Neil Paynter

wild goose
publications

www.**ionabooks**.com

Published 2017 by
Wild Goose Publications
21 Carlton Court, Glasgow G5 9JP, UK,
the publishing division of the Iona Community.
Scottish Charity No. SC003794. Limited Company Reg. No. SC096243.

ISBN 978-1-84952-548-0

Cover photo © Loreena | Dreamstime.com

Overseas distribution
Australia: Willow Connection Pty Ltd, Unit 4A, 3–9 Kenneth Road,
Manly Vale, NSW 2093
New Zealand: Pleroma, Higginson Street, Otane 4170, Central Hawkes Bay
Canada: Bayard Distribution, 10 Lower Spadina Ave., Suite 400, Toronto,
Ontario M5V 2Z

Printed by Bell & Bain, Thornliebank, Glasgow

MIX
Paper from
responsible sources
FSC® C007785

Contents

Introduction   9

Computer/smartphone prayer   13

Sixfold thanks   13

God of justice   14

Prayer for starting an engine   15

Daily walk   15

Laundry prayer   16

Cash machine prayer   16

A prayer of thanks for a cornershop   17

A plastic fiver   19

Prayer for Advent   21

Thanksgiving for a newborn child's first cry   22

Your mystery   23

Christmas intercession   24

Prayer for refugees and all in peril on the sea   26

Prayer of thanksgiving for the people of Govan   27

O Trinity of love   30

To catch me by surprise   31

O Ancient of Days   32

Keeping you at arm's length   33

Light   34

Prayer for self-knowledge   36

Dark skies (the stars are still there)   38

Prayer after unseasonable storms   39

Climate change   40

A prayer on a rainy morning   41

Welly boot prayer   41

A prayer for a wounded world   42

Three creation collects   43

Two prayers from Alaska   44

This sacramental moment
(a prayer of confession and adoration)   46

We thank you for your glory
(a prayer for Transfiguration Sunday)   48

Prayer for a youth group   50

A prayer in two parts   51

A chaplain's prayers   52

Prayer for families   54

Your healing touch   55

My name is suffering   56

Suffering Christ   57

Lament   58

Those who carry your cross today   60

God of every race and tongue   60

I believe in love: an affirmation   61

Prayer for peace, freedom and love   63

The beautiful tapestry of all creation   64

With words of peace (an Easter prayer)   66

Prayer pieces following the election of Donald Trump   68

In crisis   77

Liberating Lord   78

A prayer for ourselves and others   79

Stand with us   80

The vision of a kingdom   80

Prayer for writers   82

Unsaid words   83

The poets brought us hope   84

God's Word   85

Heaven shall not wait
(an affirmation from the MacLeod Centre)   86

Table-setting prayer   87

A psalm from the Abbey kitchen   88

Harvest supper prayer   89

Prayer for Rogation Sunday   90

Prayers for when I can't pray   91

We bring you everything, and tip it out in front of you
(intercessions for an evening service)   94

Go well: a meditation for coming times   96

I would have my heart   97

The Good Shepherd   98

A repertoire of prayers   99

You go before us   101

With your justice and peace at its heart
(a prayer for the Iona Community)   103

Sources and acknowledgements   104

About the authors   105

Introduction

Roddy Cowie, who wrote the prayer from which this book takes its title (p.94), says:

'The phrase "We bring you everything, and tip it out in front of you" comes from the picture Psalm 32 sets up in my head. Verse 5 says: "I acknowledged my sin to you, and did not cover up my wrongdoing." God's response is in verse 1: the transgressions are forgiven, and the sins are "covered". I can't help seeing the psalmist opening himself up like a duffel bag, and letting all his nasty secrets tumble out onto the floor; and God looking at the heap, and nodding, and dropping a big, heavy tarpaulin on it. Gone … '

A friend of mine has a 'prayer jar', stuffed with scraps of paper with the names of people and situations in the world written on them: refugees and asylum seekers fleeing war-torn countries, the war in Syria … During his discipline of daily prayer he takes 'random' scraps from the jar and prays for that person or concern. Some nights, tips the jar out and lights a candle on his shelf. He says: 'The initial writing of the names is prayer also. And then I give the person or situation over to God, into God's hands.'

Thom Shuman, a pastor and associate of the Iona Community in Ohio, and another contributor to this book, keeps a 'manna jar':

'Usually it's stuck up on the top shelf of the bookcase next to my desk ... Well, actually it's not a jar, but a Sainsbury's Assorted Biscuits tin from England. And instead of being filled with delicious treats (which are long gone!), it is filled with 'manna', that bread of heaven, all those gifts from God to remind me that I am God's beloved child.

There are cards from families thanking me for funerals, weddings or baptisms which I have done; there are crayoned notes from children, who now have children of their own; there is a picture of my mother, taken when she was much younger; there are e-mails from friends and colleagues; there is a ribbon which wrapped chocolate that a dear friend brought back to me from France; there is a stone from Lindisfarne, some sand from Martyrs' Bay on Iona, a rock from Omaha Beach, a pressed flower from Taizé ...

They are reminders of places where God has led me, people with whom God has graced me, all the gifts God has poured out upon me over the years. They are, as the liturgy puts it, "outward and visible signs" of that invisible and spiritual bread of life God gives to us each and every day, if we only take notice.

When I am spinning and whirling from a life of stress, I open my manna jar and breathe the sweet aroma of the Spirit's healing presence, and it seems my hyperventilating soul begins

*to calm; when the demands of ministry have stripped me bare,
I touch the words, the paper, the stones – all those inanimate
objects that put sinew and muscle back onto my dried bones;
when I hunger for a friend, an affirmation, a reminder that
God loves me and cares for me, I feast upon these tender
sweets, and my emptiness is filled to overflowing, my broken
spirit is made whole. And I put the lid back on my manna jar,
and continue on through the wilderness.'* [1]

In the *Carmina Gadelica*, Alexander Carmichael's 19th-century col-
lection of prayers from the Gaelic-speaking regions of Scotland,
there are blessings for kindling and smooring the fire, and prayers
to the sun, moon and stars; prayers for waking and sleeping, and
for birth and death; prayers for God's protection and the healing
of the soul, and for sprained ankles and indigestion; prayers for
home and hearth, and for leaving on long journeys – prayers for
*the whole of life. 'Either Christ is the Lord of all, or He is not Lord at
all,'* said founder of the Iona Community, George MacLeod.

Here, in that same 'Celtic' tradition, is a prayer for starting an
engine, and prayers to keep us engaged and on the road to God's
Kingdom; a prayer for taking a daily walk, and a prayer for refugees
travelling dangerous seas; an Iona Abbey kitchen prayer for chopping carrots, making bread and sanitising surfaces, and a Harvest
supper prayer of sharing; prayers for personal healing, and prayers
for our deeply wounded world; a prayer for self-knowledge, and
another for doing the laundry and remembering 'lost socks' –

prayers, and a few poems, too,[2] for *the whole of life*, tumbled out of our duffel-bag hearts and left in a tip at God's feet …

… And now we pause a while in silence, waiting for you to show us what we need to understand …[3]

Neil Paynter, Biggar, Scotland, 2017

Notes:

1. From *Bare Feet and Buttercups: Resources for Ordinary Time*, Ruth Burgess (Ed.), Wild Goose Publications, 2008

2. I have included a few poems because I think for many folk the discipline of reading and writing poetry is prayerful. A moment of communion: of being fed, nourished and inspired. *'As members of the Iona Community we commit ourselves to: daily prayer, worship with others and regular engagement with the Bible and other material which nourishes us'* (From the Rule of the Iona Community).

3. From the prayer 'We bring you everything, and tip it out in front of you (intercessions for an evening service)', by Roddy Cowie, p.94

Computer/Smartphone prayer

As I connect with others
bring me closer to you
and further from all that seeks to harm.

David McNeish

Sixfold thanks

God of the sunlight, thank you for the gift
of being able to respond to light.

God of the living breath, thank you for the gift
of being able to feel it brush our skin.

God of the sunset, thank you for the gift
of sharing in the cycles of time.

God of the stars, thank you for the gift
of being able to discern the pattern in their courses.

God of the darkness, thank you for the gift
of being able to sleep in peace.

God of our inner selves, thank you
from the silence of our souls.
Amen

Roddy Cowie

God of justice

Loving generous God of justice,
while we rejoice in and thank you for
our many, many blessings,
we also recognise that we are part of an unjust world order.

As we thank you for our friends and families,
we pray for those who are lonely,
those in solitary confinement or who,
feeling misunderstood,
isolate themselves from others.

We thank you for our homes, secure shelter, comfortable beds
and we pray for the homeless, rough-sleepers,
those in inadequate housing,
for refugees and displaced persons
and those living in fear.

We thank you for our freedom to speak out politically
and to worship as we choose,
and we pray for prisoners of conscience, victims of torture,
of slavery, exploitation and oppression.

We pray for the perpetrators of violence,
and for those who work for peace, justice and freedom.
Help us to give thanks always (and without guilt).

May our thankfulness fuel our compassion –
and our compassion spur us to action.

Frances Hawkey

Prayer for starting an engine

As I start this engine
may I not start without you.
Guard me, guide me
and fuel all my endeavours.

David McNeish

Daily walk*

God, thank you for bringing me to this new day.
Help me to walk at your pace,
to meet you in others,
to receive what you offer,
and to rest in your love.

* Can substitute 'work' for 'walk' and 'us' for 'me'.

David Osborne

Laundry prayer

God of every lost sock,
bless _____.
May they walk in peace,
and tread gently upon the earth.

David McNeish

Cash machine prayer

All-giving God,
as I withdraw cash,
let me not withdraw from you.
Grant me a generous heart,
content to spend itself on you.
Amen

David McNeish

A prayer of thanks for a Cornershop

You're not even on the corner.
You're under the tenements, opposite the church,
between the scruffy blue door of number 19
and the Bookies at 23.
But you're there, available, open when I need you.
I give thanks for you, cornershop.

You always seem to have what I need.
Your delicious samosas, my comfort food;
disposable nappies when I'm the designated shopper;
the bread, and milk, and rolls, and toilet paper.
No point in asking, 'How much?'
You're my friend, cornershop.

Your two custodians are delightful.
I don't know their names – and they've never asked mine –
but we always greet each other like long-lost friends.
It's what regulars do, in a cornershop.
Customer-care comes naturally. I like that.
I smile when I enter you, cornershop.

You were open on Christmas Day.
I needed you then – when everything else was closed.
It was for chipolata sausages, the ones I forgot.
And you had some, thank God,

in the cool-cabinet – my festive rescue-remedy.
You've been my saviour, cornershop.

You don't ask where I've come from or am rushing to.
You're just the same, when I'm irritable, grumpy, or happy.
You welcome me, as I am, in all my searching.
I admire you, cornershop.

You're the most inclusive place I know,
open, welcoming, friendly, non-judgemental ...
The church across the road could learn from you.
Keep showing what matters, just as you've always done.
We've got a lot to admire you for.
Good stuff, cornershop.

I hope you're going to stay around for a while.
Don't worry about Tesco Metros and Sainsbury's Locals.
I pray to God you'll still be here,
like a blue door, and a bookies, and a church.
I'll never take you for granted.
Because I love you – cornershop.

Tom Gordon

A plastic fiver

A new one,
bluish, plastic, pristine,
a fiver in my hand,
flash,
ready to be stored away safely.

I don't like you, plastic fiver –
no personality, no life,
this fiver in my hand,
different,
not like the others at all.

Look! Here's your old cousin!
Not yet 'out of service',
this fiver in my hand;
useful,
ready to help the world go round.

I like *you*, wrinkled as you are.
There's history in your grubbiness,
old fiver in my hand.
Life,
well-lived, for a long time.

Well done, old man.
You've had your good days.

A fiver in my hand
again,
as you've been in the hands of many others.

What hands have held you?
What good have you done,
this fiver in my hand,
success,
alone or with others over the years?

What stories have you to tell?
What places have you been,
this fiver in my hand?
Well-travelled?
Or have I met you before and don't recall?

I like you – more than your plastic pal.
You're like me, aren't you,
fiver in my hand?
A life,
with still much to do, much good to do.

You'll have your time,
bluish, plastic, pristine
fiver in my hand.
Eventually …
But you've no story to share with me yet.

Tom Gordon

Prayer for Advent

Lord Jesus, you came as light into the midst
of a people who walked in darkness.
We remember today especially those who suffer injustice,
poverty and violence …

Lord Jesus, you came as the Prince of Peace
born into a country under occupation.
We remember today those who live under occupation
or in refugee camps …

Lord Jesus, you came as Saviour of all,
bringing good news of great joy for all people.
We remember today our task to continue
your saving work in the world,
until your kingdom finally and fully comes,
for which we pray, saying …

Lord's Prayer …

Richard Sharples

Thanksgiving for a newborn Child's first Cry

Speeches move nations,
words draw lovers closer.
Silence can express a peace between enemies.
Apologies can heal great pain –
but nothing, nothing,
prepared me for the utter joy of hearing
your first cry, my child.

Thanks, oh joyful thanksgiving,
to the power that brings new life into being –
into our arms and into our hearts.

Ewan Aitken

Your mystery

You called it all into being:
this expanding universe that keeps growing.
I cannot number the stars
and even less can I number the planets that circle them.
The whole is governed by laws of physics
that we humans are still discovering.
The more of Your mystery You reveal –
the more amazed we are.
Perhaps our greatest joy is to realise
that You have chosen us on
this one small planet
at the edge of the universe
to be the ones who receive bits and pieces
of Your mystery as a continuing revelation.
Certainly a great revelation is Your coming among us
as an infant One of us who gives us the gift of resurrection.
How can we thank You,
except by loving and accepting one another.
Amen

Israel Nelson

Christmas intercession

God our Father,
we think of Jesus' parents looking for shelter for the night,
and pray for those who are homeless …

We think of Jesus born in a stable,
and pray for all who live in poverty …

We think of shepherds on the hills at night,
and pray for all who are separated from their friends or families …

We think of wise men following a star,
and pray for all who are searching for light in their darkness
or meaning in their confusion …

We think of Herod and his advisers
troubled at the news of Jesus' birth,
and pray for all who have great power …

We think of Jesus and his parents fleeing to Egypt,
and pray for all who seek safety from violence or persecution,
or healing from injury …

O God, we think of your presence among us in Jesus Christ:

Let those who are troubled
know you suffer with them in their anxiety, pain or confusion;

let those who struggle for peace and justice
know that you are beside them;

let those who seek love
know that you are with them;

let those who seek healing
know that you work within them;

let those who have power over others
know that you stand before them;

and may we all have
the wisdom,
the strength,
the love,
the peace
and the hope
that are your gifts to us
in Jesus Christ, our Lord.

David Osborne

Prayer for refugees and all in peril on the sea

I grew up in the naval town of Rosyth, my father working in the dockyard. So the navy hymn 'Eternal Father, strong to save' was sung often. My grandfather had served at the Battle of Jutland and my father-in-law on the Arctic convoys. I spent most of my working life in Aberdeen, where the risks borne by both the traditional fishing and the offshore oil workers were very real. Recently we lived in Malta, supporting the work of rescuing migrants and helping those who settled there (Out of Africa into Malta: www.standrewsmalta.com/out-of-africa-into-malta; Migrant Offshore Aid Station: https://www.moas.eu). Attending a funeral for the many migrants who had drowned in one of the worst of such incidents will stay with me always, especially seeing the white coffin for the boy who died.

Eternal Father, strong to save,
today we pray for all in peril on the sea.
We remember those serving in the navy
and the merchant fleet;
fishermen;
those working offshore in the oil industry;
lifeboat crews; and others.

We especially pray for those desperate refugees,
men, women and children,

fleeing conflict and persecution,
risking their lives crossing the Mediterranean
in unsafe boats,
and for those working on the rescue ships,
saving them from drowning.

Peter Lloyd

Prayer of thanksgiving for the people of Govan

(From the Service of thanksgiving and commitment on the 75th anniversary of the founding of the Iona Community, 2015)

Living God,
Creator, Son and Spirit,
you have shown yourself to us
as a community of love,
offered to your whole creation
as a model for fullness of life.

Today we give special thanks
for this community of Govan,
so central to the life of the Iona Community
over these many years.

We thank you
that through all the centuries

of change, of growth, of struggle, of success and failure,
there rang throughout this community
the hammer-sounds of solidarity,
of resilience, of strong civic pride –
sounds which have been heard
with renewed resonance
in these last days.

We thank you
that from the very beginning of this community of Govan,
the Gospel was heard here –
lived and proclaimed by Celtic monks,
Roman priests, Reformed ministers,
and countless numbers of men, women and children –
and is still lived and heard
even now, in these challenging times,
helping, as in all the years gone by,
to support, form and challenge the people,
the families, the society of this place.

Especially do we thank you today
for the gifts this community of Govan
has given to the Iona Community
over these 75 years:

through the life-changing ministry
of our founder, George MacLeod;

through the men and women of Govan
who have helped to form the Iona Community
over the decades;
through the worship of this parish church,
so influential in forming the worship on Iona
in so many ways;
through the Pearce Institute,
a resting-place and a powerhouse
for our work in Glasgow and far beyond.

In love and gratitude,
on this special day,
we commend this community of Govan
to your continuing care and guidance,
in its heart, its body and its soul,
in the name of the Trinity of Love,
God the Creator,
Christ the Redeemer,
Spirit the Enabler,
now and forever. Amen

John Harvey

O Trinity of love

O Trinity of love,
our model and our friend,
you live in love with difference –
community in persons
in endless harmony.

You seek to help us love
with difference
for different folk in different lands and tongues
and circumstance that shapes
their story and the ways we serve.
Our neighbours here today
are trafficked children, hungry families,
the wounded seeking hope, young men in boats
adrift, disowned and thirsty, driven by fear,
then spurned as flotsam, but your gift.

Help us to see the ones you call us to,
flawed like ourselves but holding in their souls
a shard of your creative love,
immortal diamond, Eden's light,
shining through darkness,
lighting our journeys,
drawing us back through others
to our deepest self, to your abiding home.

Rosemary Power

To catch me by surprise

Holy Spirit,
You appear in some of the strangest places
and at the strangest times.
You introduce me to a child on my street
who shares my birthday.
Is that You inviting me to share my first book –
a birthday gift from a favourite teacher –
and thereby spark interest in learning?
Years ago I met someone in a prison ministry programme
and now that person is my neighbour.
Is there really coincidence
or are You merely hiding in the obvious?
Slowly I am learning how You direct the course of my life.
Please continue to catch me by surprise
and thereby renew my faith
in Your loving leadership of my being.
Amen

Israel Nelson

O Ancient of Days

O Ancient of Days, God of wonder and might,
remind us that we are made for days such as these.

Increase our courage and strength and fortitude.
Increase our grace and humour and trust.

Through Abraham and Sarah,
you taught us to receive the stranger into our homes.

Through the laws you gave to Moses,
you taught us to practise hospitality.

And through the life of Jesus,
you demonstrated the walk of the faithful with the scapegoats,
the marginalised, the oppressed.

May we continue to walk the path towards you,
and continue to resist those who diss hospitality
in favour of 'security' as a way to anchor greed or prejudice.
Do not let us silence our voice.
Do not let us silence the voices of others.

To you we bring all of our hopes and sorrows,
all of our fears and anxieties,
all of our faith and love.

May we serve you, O Ancient of Days,
to the best of our being.
In the name of Jesus, we pray.
Amen

Lisa Bodenheim

Keeping you at arm's length

Brother Jesus,
through the centuries we have focused our attention
mostly on how You are wholly God.
We are not sure how we should react to Your nature
as one of us.
So long as we are able to keep You at arm's length,
we can excuse our failures to be all that we can be,
all that You call us to be.
We can continue to fail to accept one another,
making enemies and fighting wars.
After all, we are only human and not God!
But You came to us as a human baby,
born in poverty and ethnic alienation.
You endured the doubts of those
who should have recognised You.
At the end, You cried out from torture,
'My God, my God, why have you forsaken me?'

And then You called us all into Resurrection.
Don't give up on us.
Keep calling us.
Redeem us all, brothers and sisters,
through the power of love.
Amen

Israel Nelson

Light

Living God,
I'm confused.
I would like to be offering you
a life more together –
but the longer I live,
the less perfect it feels.
And I would dearly wish
to be living in a world
more perfectly mirroring
the values of your kingdom –
but in most places just now
these are not what I'm seeing.

Forgive me if my eyes
are too dull,
and my looking too cynical.
But thank you
for reminding me
that *'there is a crack in everything:*
that's how the light gets in'.*
Please keep me looking for that crack
in my life
and in the life of the world;
please keep me ever open
to the Light that still shines,
even in the darkness,
which can never put it out.

I pray, through Jesus Christ.
Amen

John Harvey

* Leonard Cohen, from 'Anthem'

Prayer for Self-knowledge

Father of light,
we ask for light to see ourselves without deception.
Pierce through the fictions that we weave about ourselves –
casting ourselves as heroes when we manage to step onto
the good ground in front of us,
and victims when we blunder
into the bog beside it;
eager to think that we know everything that matters in the world
against the towering evidence of our own ignorance
and short-sightedness;
contemptuous of the best that other people can do,
oblivious of the fact that we could do no better;
easily swept up in the passionate belief
that we can make things right by hitting out,
with no idea how to rebuild after the anger fades;
claiming to witness to the world for Christ,
but far too stiff to give ourselves to love
in the way he showed us was possible.

Father of light,
pierce through the fictions that we weave about ourselves.
And when we stand in front of you,
with all our shadowy falsehoods brushed aside by light,
let us see that beneath them is a creature that you love;

and who, however weakly and brokenly,
reflects a fragment of the image of its maker;
then let us look to one side and the other,
and see how those on either side
also reflect your light.
We ask it in the name of Jesus Christ,
your son, Light of the world.
Amen

Roddy Cowie

Dark skies (the stars are still there)

From where we are, it's hard to see the stars.
They are still there, though; we've just
dazzled ourselves with all these lesser lights,
so now we can't see wood for trees,
or glimpse God among us. It's such a waste:
glitter and glare dim the dance of eternity.
But don't lose hope: the stars are still there.

The same with sounds: hard now to hear
what really matters: election rhetoric,
religious jargon, and our own empty chat
all deafen us. Yet out there in the cold,
beyond borders, listen – a singing silence
and a newborn baby's cry –
now can you hear the music of the spheres?

Light pollution confuses: what's left to lose?
Ask: is the blackness total, are there cracks?
Surrender to the huge darkness of these skies –
they will not eat you.

Look up now, do not fear;
small mortal being, you are not alone.
So let the scales fall from your eyes
and be amazed: the stars are still there.

Jan Sutch Pickard

Prayer after unseasonable storms

Lord Jesus, we have seen signs in the sky –
thunder and lightning and the rain flooding the streets.
We know that these are signs of changes in the earth itself
and that there is little time for humanity to slow the change
before the icecaps melt,
the seas rise
and the deserts grow.
Lord Christ, bless our foolish race
that has balanced the future of the world on a knife edge;
and show us, your disciples in this age,
what we can do about it.

Let us not see our world in danger
and close our eyes;
let us not miss the opportunities
brought by your grace
to make humanity a better steward of this world you set us in.
We ask it in the name of Jesus,
whose word tells us that God loves the world.
Amen

Roddy Cowie

Climate Change

O God, Creator of all that is –
of seas and clouds, rain and rivers,
grass and trees, insects and fish,
humans, animals, birds and reptiles,
of all life connected, sharing this one earth –
we are aware that our way of living
is profoundly affecting the earth's climate,
that many people are in danger of flood or drought,
that some are greatly impoverished,
and the whole fabric of life is in danger;

to those who make international policies,
give wisdom and courage;
to those who direct industry and commerce,
give a concern for the common good;
to those who struggle for justice,
give strength and hope;
and to us all
give the grace to change our ways
for the good of all that lives
and for your glory.
Amen

David Osborne

A prayer on a rainy morning

If *'This is the day that the good Lord has made'*,
then why has it started with rain?
If you're in control like we're taught to believe,
I pray that you'll try once again –
to get the day off to a half-decent start.
Lord, let your mistake be undone!
If this is the day that you've made just for us,
please, God – start it off with some sun!

Tom Gordon

Welly boot prayer

Protect me from the gutter,
and keep my feet planted in the earth,
even as I look to the heavens.

David McNeish

A prayer for a wounded world

Dear Lord,

thank you for this world of
beauty, diversity and creation.

We are sorry that we damage it with
pollution, isolation and destruction.

Sometimes we wound the world with our
conflict, greed and hate.

Please help us to heal it with
peace, kindness and love.

Amen

Kerry Davies

Three Creation Collects

I

Creator God,
by your word you call all things into being
and reveal yourself within your world;
open our eyes to see your glory
and our ears to hear your word,
and give us the strength to follow the way of Jesus Christ,
your Word made flesh.

II

Almighty God,
you create this earth as a place of great abundance;
give us the wisdom to enjoy its goodness,
to share its wealth,
and to serve you in all we do,
through Jesus Christ our Lord.

III

Creator God,
you make us in your image from the dust of the earth;
by your Spirit give us grace to seek your justice,
to share your peace and to show your love,
made known in Jesus Christ our Lord.

David Osborne

Two prayers from Alaska

Being tempted to join Brother Grizzly

In the dark cold of winter,
I am tempted to join Brother Grizzly in hibernation.
When it is dark and cold
I seem only able to feel my failures
and my attention is drawn more to the folly of human efforts
to tame the feared chaos.
But in the dark and cold You are working a miracle:
the return of sunlight showing
the wild profusion of renewed life –
the resurrection of the world.

Like the darkness, the light comes every year.
Please help me, Miracle of Light,
to grasp the promise
and wait for the Light
that the darkness cannot overcome.
Amen

Your abundant grace

Thank You for the forest that provides wood to heat my cabin.
Thank You for the salmon that ends my hunger.
Thank You for the Aurora on cold, clear winter nights
which fills the sky with dancing colour
and reminds me that,
even when You seem most distant,
You are still watching over me.
I praise You for Sister Moose
who gives me meat for food and hide for boots.
Thank You for Brother Bear
who supplies me with meat for my table and fur for my coat.
You supply my needs with abundance.
Amen

Israel Nelson

This sacramental moment

(a prayer of confession and adoration)

Somewhere, sometime, Lord, long ago,
perhaps in Sunday school days,
or listening to a television quiz,
or tripping upon it in a novel,
or a long-forgotten poem …
somewhere we stumbled upon that rare and mysterious word …
'sacrament'.

Like an adult picking up a shell on a beach,
perhaps we weren't sure what we had found,
but it was too beautiful to ignore.
Unsure what it meant,
unsure what its purpose was,
yet we gathered it up … 'sacrament'.

And it became part of our vocabulary:
perhaps a rare word,
a Sunday word,
a poetic word,
but it was there.

Perhaps we have never written it,
possibly we have never spoken it,
but it is there …
it is part of how we see the world.

Hopefully. Curiously. Sacramentally.
Still looking for gold amongst the dross.

Perhaps, Lord, it is a key to unlocking our world …
A 'sacramental moment', so we are told,
is when something ordinary appears to us to be extra-ordinary.

The everyday sunset which on this occasion stuns us into silence.
The granddaughter's lisped 'love you, granny'
is pure and true as the first day of Eden.
The still-wet lamb with the stuttering legs
draws from us an involuntary gasp
which the angels know is praise.
The spring garlic which turns a verge
into a scented orchard.

And here, now,
the chattering of gathering disciples and restless searchers,
in this place of quarried stone and crafted wood
and rainbow glass.
We are gentled into silence
because this, Lord, is our prayer,
this is holy nakedness;
this is to bow before our Maker …

… and to wait for healing, for forgiveness, for hope …
for those glimpses of eternity which alone make sense
of our wretched and wonderful mortal moments.

Thank you, Lord, for bringing us here,
to this sacramental moment,
for we will surely leave richer than we arrived.
And with that inheritance
which grace alone gives,
may our lives be a blessing for others,
a source of comfort and laughter,
of gentleness and generosity.
And so the Kingdom comes,
even through folk like us ... Amen

Ewen Gilchrist

We thank you for your glory
(a prayer for Transfiguration Sunday)

Lord,
today we thank you for the privilege of knowing your glory.
We thank you for your glory in the storms
that hurled over us in winter.

We thank you for your glory in the light of the sun
breaking through again as winter ends.
We thank you for your glory in this lovely church,
made lovelier by your light

in all its colours
streaming through the windows.

We thank you for your glory
in the green life that surges up again.

We thank you for your glory reflected in the human race –
the energy and beauty of youth,
the dignified beauty of age.

Above all on this day
we thank you for the greater glory
that the disciples saw when Jesus stood high on a mountain
and shone with the first dawn of the eternal light.

Lord, bring us at the last into the full glory
that you prepared for us and all your children
before the beginning of all the worlds.
Through Jesus Christ our Lord.
Amen

Roddy Cowie

Prayer for a youth group

In all that baffles and surprises,
God walk with us on the journey of our lives.

In the injustice and unfairness that surrounds us,
God walk with us on the journey of our lives.

When no one will listen and nothing seems to change,
God walk with us on the journey of our lives.

When we long for a better, fairer world,
God walk with us on the journey of our lives.

Give us the courage we need to be part of the solutions.
God walk with us on the journey of our lives.

David McNeish

A prayer in two parts

O my God …
I curse the cancer that grew in my body
I curse the surgery that has changed my body
I curse the radiation that has burned my body
I curse the chemicals that poisoned my body and my brain …

O my God …
I am blessed by the freedom to be angry
I am blessed by the gift of more life
I am blessed by the healing gifts
you placed in the hands of the surgeon
I am blessed by all those
who brought their knowledge to help me
I am blessed by all those who held my hand
I am blessed by all the encouragers
who could laugh and pray with me
I am blessed by the old friend who said,
'We're not letting you go!'
You have blessed me.
Amen

Andrew Foster

A Chaplain's prayers

Compassionate God

Compassionate God, today many people will find themselves in hospital, because of sudden illness or injury, a long-term illness getting worse, or for minor or major surgery. Be with them in their worry, pain and confusion. Take away their fear and assure them they are surrounded by care and competence. May they know your healing love through good and bad days, and your promise that, no matter what happens, 'all will be well'.

We pray this in the name of the one who turned suffering into salvation, Jesus Christ our Lord. Amen

Caring God

Caring God, today and tonight many people will go to work as paramedics, nurses, doctors, specialists and support staff. May they be assured that, in all they do and say, they can bring healing care to those they meet. Give them the grace to see through anxiety and anger to the human suffering within, and do their utmost to restore peace of mind to all those they encounter in their work, to bring people back to good health, and to stand mercifully by others in their dying hours.

We ask this in the name of the one who never turned away from those who suffered, and restored many to health of body, mind and spirit, Jesus Christ our Lord. Amen

God our father and mother, brother and friend

God our father and mother, brother and friend, today many people will realise they have gradually or suddenly become carers for someone they love dearly. Standing helpless by the bed of suffering, struggling to nurse and care for someone at home, or to stay in touch with someone in a nursing home or hospice, may they find assurance that they are not alone; may they seek the help and support they need and, with thankful hearts, accept the help that others offer. Give them grace to find ways to communicate with their loved one and to find time and space just to be themselves.

We pray this in the name of the one who gave his mother and his friend to love and care for each other even in his dying agony, Jesus Christ our Lord. Amen

Anna Briggs

Prayer for families

Almighty God,
you watch over us; you neither slumber nor sleep.
You know full well the triumphs
and the tragedies of our own families.
The love and the loss, the delights and the disagreements.
The words harshly spoken, and those not spoken at all.

God of Abraham, Isaac and Jacob,
draw near to those families
who even today feel like there is too much to contend with.
Families in the midst of the pain of separation.
Families fractured by love gone sour.
We pray for those contending with illness and infirmity.
Families worried by test results and procedures yet to come.
Families whose dreams are being reshaped
by circumstances they dread.

We pray too for families in which there are long-standing hurts.
Rifts shored up by silence and resentment.
Let your healing be at work in these families,
in our families, in the families of those we know,
and in the families we have never met.
Let your forgiveness be released
on all whose fists are tightly clenched.
Let your mercy triumph over all who sit in judgement.

God you show your love to every generation;
you work through families we might well give up on.
You work through us.

Let your mercy and compassion be the hallmarks of our lives.
And may your dreams save us all.
In Christ's name we pray.
Amen

David McNeish

Your healing touch

Dear Lord,
you know my heart and my intentions.
And sometimes I act wrongly.
Be near today to those I have betrayed or let down.
You know them and I know them.
Help me to see that we all stand in need of grace.
Help me not to run away from my own failures
and to accept deep down
that I, too, need your healing touch today.

Peter Millar

My name is Suffering

My name is suffering
I am broken
I am nothing
I am frozen
I am wounded
I am in the depths
Where are you?
Why do you hide?
Why when I need hope do you disappear?
Why when I need that friend are you not there?
I cry out to you … I hear silence
So loud is the quietness
Where are you?
My pain is too difficult to bear
I can't do this on my own, Lord
I need you
I need you
I need you

And finally you whisper
Wisdom
into my battered mind
into my broken heart

I love you
I'm here

You are mine
You are safe
Rest in me
Hope in me.

Rev. Liz England

Suffering Christ

When trust is broken
and love betrayed,
help us, incorruptible Christ,
to face another day.
When we are judged unworthy,
judged inadequate,
and told we are not good enough,
help us, forgiving Christ,
to find the courage
to live another day.

When we are ignored and forgotten,
help us,
suffering Christ,
to know you.
Amen

Susan Lindsay

Lament

A prayer from Iona following the terrorist attack in Nice on Bastille Day 2016

20 confirmed dead.
The wind howls and moans
into every nook and crevice
as our hearts break, once again.

40 confirmed dead.
The rain pours down, echoing our falling tears,
adding to an ocean of sorrow.

60 confirmed dead.
Miles and miles and miles away
strangers lives broken, torn,
just holding together with fragile threads.

And we lament.
Mothers, fathers, sisters, brothers,
aunts, uncles, cousins, friends …

We lament, and our tiny piece of paradise
laments with us.

Then, slowly, gently, gracefully,
without us really noticing,

the wind will lift the pall
from around the shoulders of our paradise.
And the sun will shine again.

We *must* be changed by this.
We *are* changed by this.
As the shadows on the ground lengthen
and strengthen, we remember that we are called
by a light that shines in darkness.

As we see again familiar shores and mountaintops
we remember that darkness
will not overcome the light that calls us.
And we will be sent out.
We will pray more earnestly.
We will live more authentically.
We will love more fiercely.

And miles and miles and miles away,
know you are in our prayers tonight.
And every night.

Emily D'Silva, member of the Resident Group on Iona

Those who Carry your Cross today

Lord, as I think of your Cross,
give me courage and grace,
not only for myself but to be able to visualise
those who carry a cross today.
Let me be near those who are tortured and abused;
those who are abandoned;
those who walk alone;
those who are being robbed of their dignity;
those who only know war;
and those who are being killed
because they believe in you.

Peter Millar

God of every race and tongue

God of every race and tongue,
may the peoples of our world learn again
to be humble enough to listen to one another
instead of rushing to easy judgements.
To be humble enough to admit to error.
To have the gift of humility
which enables the other to flourish
as well as ourselves.

Peter Millar

I believe in love: an affirmation

On 12th June 2016, 49 people died and 53 were wounded in a mass shooting at Pulse, an LGBT nightclub in Orlando, Florida. A few days later, on 16th June 2016, Jo Cox, MP for Batley and Spen, West Yorkshire, died after being shot and stabbed multiple times whilst on a street of her constituency. This piece was written in response to these events.

I believe in love
that lifts the heart like skylark's flight,
and grounds the soul in earth's deep song.

I believe in the tender love
of teenage kids on a playground swing,
who share a Coke and a bag of chips,
while from his pocket the boy pulls a coin
to carve a heart on an ancient tree.

I believe in the unlikely love
that breaches borders and battlelines.
Where curse and clash of conflict reigns
love cracks convention,
sowing seeds of hope
in the wasted lands of war.

And I believe in boy meets girl,
and girl meets girl
and boy meets boy;

and I believe in love that stands
with tear-soaked eyes and grief-gripped soul,
where hate and fear have gunned down young lives,
to hold aloft a fragile flame
of solidarity and strength.

I believe in a woman's love,
who dared to build a place of peace
within the streets where she grew up,
only to be cut down by cruel hands.

Still, I believe in love which heals
and holds and faces fear full on.
Generous love that lifts the heart like skylark's flight,
and grounds the soul in earth's deep song.

Elaine Gisbourne

Prayer for peace, freedom and love

Life-giving God,
you have made a beautiful world
of blue skies and green fields,
of sunlight and birdsong,
of music and laughter.
You have made us all
to live in peace with one another.
But there is not enough peace in the world.
We pray for peace …
We pray for peace in Syria,
peace in the Middle East, peace in Israel and Palestine.
Peace in our homes and peace in our hearts.

You have made us to live in freedom.
But there is not enough freedom in the world.
We pray for freedom …
Freedom for refugees, freedom for prisoners, freedom for slaves.
Freedom in our homes and freedom in our hearts.

You have made us to live in love.
But there is not enough love in the world.
We pray for love …
Love for the bereaved, love for the sick, love for the lonely.
Love in our homes and love in our hearts.

Loving Christ,
you come to bring us peace and freedom and love.
You make us your people.
Clothe us in truth and righteousness.
Give us sturdy shoes to walk the paths of peace
in the troubled places of the world.
Give us words of freedom.
Keep us faithful,
keep us prayerful.

Lord's Prayer …

Susan Miller

The beautiful tapestry of all Creation

God of infinite variety,
of many threads and textures,
we give thanks for the world that is our home.
A world where a little child,
pink with effort of her first breath,
is gently welcomed
by the brown skilled hands of the midwife.
And a black child
is helped to birth by kind white hands.

Ever-creating God,
help us to see the richness in the diversity
you have offered to us.
Make us welcomers,
sharing what we have and who we are.
For we then might receive the privilege
of being welcomed by others.

Sometimes, we will be challenged,
for in this world around us, so rich in possibilities,
we see prejudice and injustice,
greed and misuse of power.
We see the creation of artificial barriers of race.
Instead of celebrating our common humanity,
we become territorial.
We talk about 'us' and 'ours',
and 'theirs' and 'them'.

Teach us to see difference as opportunity.
Let us live in the loom of your creation
as threads of many colours
which together make up
a beautiful tapestry –
the tapestry of all creation.

Isabel Whyte

With words of peace (an Easter prayer)

In the evening when the disciples met,
frightened behind locked doors,
you came to them with words of peace.
For wicked plots had failed,
and the cruelty of the world had come to nothing,
and the betrayal and the denial of friends had not prevailed.

Life-giving God,
we give you thanks –
for Jesus has risen.
You turn darkness into light
and bring goodness out of evil
and life out of death.

In government rooms where politicians meet,
in city boardrooms where executives plan,
in courtrooms where lawyers debate,
come with words of clarity and justice.

In hospital rooms where people are waiting,
in prison cells where people are afraid,
in homes where people struggle to make ends meet,
in rooms where people grieve,
come with words of peace.

And in the silence, we bring before you
those we care for and are worried about …

Come to us with words of peace.
Despite the strong and solid doors we lock
to protect ourselves,
to shut out the world,
come to us with courage.

This Easter breathe on us again
with gentleness.
For you have overcome evil
and wicked plots fail,
and the cruelty of the world comes to nothing,
and the betrayal and the denial of friends do not prevail.

Let us be renewed in the power of your Spirit –
that we may have life in your name
and go wherever you send us.

Lord's Prayer …

Susan Miller

Prayer pieces following the election of Donald Trump

And on the eighth day,
you said:
share the light,
give everyone a cool drink,
feed those around you,
dance under the stars,
explore the skies and waters,
be gentle with every creature,
you are not alone …
… and relax – it's not all about you.

+   +

Sadly,
we have become
nightlights of
comfort so the
quo can sleep
through the night,
rather
than beacons of hope
for those suffering
from injustice,
hatred and
no status.

+   +

Forgive us when
we, who are so
graced by you,
show such bad
manners towards
those around us
who are struggling,
different,
a seeming threat.

+   +

With a hat and gloves,
we can warm
the rough-sleeper;
with a smile,
we can ease
the child's fears;
with a word,
we can cradle
the senior's loneliness;
and bring healing
to our selfish
apathy.

+   +

When we see immigrants
welcomed with joy
or

injustice brought
to its knees,
when we listen to
children speak out
against bullies,
or
the rough-sleeper invite
others to share a meal,
how
can we not run
to share this good news?

+   +

The generation which
Balkanises the playground
so everyone knows
their place and
never crosses the line,
or the one which
welcomes and teaches
games to outsiders
and learns new ones
from them ...
which shall we be?

+   +

When we hunger
to do the harder right

rather than the easier
expediency;
when our thirst
for justice will
not be quenched by
sugary platitudes;
when fairness breaks out
in the corridors of
power and
not just on
playgrounds,
we will have found your way.

+   +

They come with
dreams cradled in their
hopes:
that children can be lifted
out of poverty;
that peace could emerge
from the ashes of war;
that people just might
learn how to love each other,
and
we toss them and their dreams
in the empty bin, as
we watch reality shows
hosted by con artists

eager to fill our hollow souls
with even more emptiness.

+   +

When
we step over
the homeless on our way
to buy another
$5 coffee;
give our
cast-offs to the
shivering kids instead
of a new coat;
throw out
enough food to
feed another
family,
we have left our
compassion
back in the boat
once again.

+   +

When we wonder
if the new captain even
knows the bow
from the stern;
when we worry

that justice
will be jettisoned
over the side;
when we fear
that the vulnerable
will be left behind,
may the winds of faith
continue to refresh us,
so we may journey
with you until we reach
the shores of compassion,
inclusion,
peace and
hope.

+   +

Noticing the scarfed
teenager sitting alone
on the bus;
listening to the
immigrant child
translating for his
parents;
comforting those
who find themselves
outsiders looking in,
we meet our family,
and weep

for our loss in
not knowing them
all our lives.

+   +

We hold hoops
for the poor
to jump through,
while you make
snow angels with them;
we write regulations
enabling the hungry
to receive our leftovers,
while you take them
out for dinner;
we look down our noses
at those standing on corners
with hand-scrawled appeals,
and you offer them
a lift to your heart.

+   +

May we be
the umbrella
for those
showered by hate;
the cradling lap

for children who
tremble in the night;
the heart hollowed by grief
so we can embrace
all who have lost everything;
as you are all
this (and more)
for us.

    +   +

May hope be
not a long stare
through the poor,
but a welcome
to our tables;
nor a rueful grin
as we mime
empty pockets –
but a bear hug
of joy.
May injustice's tantalising
seductive whispers of
'They must wait their turn'
be silenced by
the singing of 'We
shall overcome'.

    +   +

When we
gorge ourselves
on pleasant
platitudes;
stuff politicians'
hollow words
down our throats;
imbibe bottle after
bottle of
fragrant whines,
is it any wonder
we feel so
empty
all the time? ...

Thom M Shuman

In Crisis

God beyond boundaries of belief and nation,
in this time of crisis we pray

for those who grieve
and those who are in pain;

those who handle weapons
and those who decide whether or when they should be used;

those who wait fearfully
and those who decide the fates of many;

those who work to bring relief to others,
and those who have influence through their words or actions.

And we pray
for peace,
that the torment of violence and fear may be overcome,

for justice,
that power in its many forms may be rightly used,

for vision,
that your way into the future may be seen,

for wisdom,
that this path may be taken,

for humility,
that pride and past wrongs may be left behind,

and for love,
that the wounds of hatred may be healed;

we pray this
believing that these are your will
for this,
your world.
Amen

David Osborne

Liberating Lord

Liberating Lord, free me –
at least sometimes during the day –
from being concerned only with myself!
Take away my inner blindness,
and help me to see that you are always calling me closer
to the One who created me
and to a new way of seeing your wonderful world
in all of its beauty and amazing diversity.

Peter Millar

A prayer for ourselves and others

Lord, who listened to those on the margins of life,
meet me in my need:
Listen with me, in my exclusion.

Lord, who overturned tables in the temple,
meet me in my need:
Speak with me, in my quest for justice.

Lord, who broke bread with friends,
meet me in my need:
Feast with me, as I celebrate today.

Lord, who wept in the Garden of Gethsemane,
meet me in my need:
Weep with me, as I weep tonight.

Lord, who walked on the water in the storm,
meet me in my need:
Stand with me, in this my darkest hour.

Lord of generosity,
meet me in my selfishness.
Teach me to put aside my own concerns
and to listen, speak, feast, weep
and stand alongside others in their need.
Amen

Susan Dale

Stand with us

Mighty God,
stand with us.
Grant us the strength
to face oppression,
not with frozen fear,
but with firm courage.
Keep us clear
on your objectives.
Touch our hearts
with your bright fire.

Chris Polhill

The vision of a kingdom

Life-giving God,
you give us the vision of a kingdom
not of diamonds and glitter,
not of success and achievement.

You give us the vision of a kingdom
not of rewards and privileges,
not of popularity and fortune.

For you sit down to eat with fishermen and tax collectors,
with the gracious and the greedy,
with the respectable and the rogues,
and you sit down with us.

Forgive us
our lack of generosity
and our lack of compassion
when we chase after pennies
and reach out for dust.
God of surprises,
God of grace,
you welcome the weak, the tired and the worn
and you welcome us.

You give us the vision of a kingdom
which turns this world upside down.
Where the first are last and the last are first.
Where the hungry are fed
and the forgotten are honoured
and the lonely are loved.

Lord's Prayer ...

Susan Miller

Prayer for writers

O Columba, hope of Scots,
hear us as we labour.

When we are called
to take the oar in hand,
put the curragh to the waves
and be wafted by words
where we would not journey
but with your Spirit.

Hear us, we pray,
when youth is strong in us
and you are our courage
as we adventure on the sea.

Hear us as we seek
for learning, like the rippling
of sunlight on calm waters.
May we remember what
you wish us to record.

Fill our sails with wind
full with yearning
for the land beyond our sight.

And hear us
when we bail the boat,
spilling the bilge that drowns.

Free us of what we want:
in work may we find your desires.

Help us on the cross
of ropes that catch the words, then bind us.
When we loathe the labour you have given us
help us weather the weariness
and come through storm
and find you before us
as you add our catch to the feast.

Rosemary Power

Unsaid words

Here I am, Jesus,
unsaid words
spinning in my head,
over and over again.
Lost in the moment,
then stuck inside.
Rewrite them, Jesus,
hear them, take them,
change the record.
Put Your words in my heart.

Chris Polhill

The poets brought us hope

Written following a poetry reading by Jackie Kay, Carol Ann Duffy,
Gillian Clarke and Imtiaz Dharker in Biggar, Scotland. At the end
of the evening, the poets held up cards saying 'Not in Our Name',
and were given a prolonged standing ovation by the audience.

The poets brought us hope,
restored our humour and
renewed our hearts,
and reminded us of who we are,
and when we marched (when millions marched)
against attacking innocents and an unjust war,
against making others less than we are,
when we stood together hand in hand
and 'Not in our name' was the chant …

Not in our name your twisted lies,
not in our name your whitewashed lives.
Not in our name your bloodstained flags,
not in our name your right-wing rags.
Not in our name your vicious acts of hate,
not in our name your words that hurt.

In our name we stand up for peace,
in our name all are valued in this place.
In our name we give roses to strangers,

in our name we celebrate our neighbours.
In our name we offer welcome and our love,
in our name we are one with all life.

The poets brought us hope.

Rachel McCann

God's Word

*Written by a group for a service in Iona Abbey on God's Word,
on a Wild Goose Publications week …*

God, help us to listen for your voice:
in the words of the Bible,
in the cries of the poor,
in the testimony of saints,
in the warnings of prophets,
in the questions of children and young people,
in everyday conversations with our neighbours,
in words unsaid,
in the movement of breath …

God, sometimes your voice may not be a voice at all.

God, help us to hear you
in the sound of the sea,

in the crash of the wind when the ferry's cancelled,
in the rustle of leaves and the sweep of a cleaning brush,
in the laughter and debate of birds in the cloisters.

Help us to sense you
in the smell of grass after a rain,
in the colours of the sea,
in the tang of salt spray,
in the touch of a stranger.
Amen

Neil Paynter and others

Heaven shall not wait
(an affirmation from the MacLeod Centre)

This affirmation came to me during a Corrymeela week on Iona in 2016; we were talking about change. It made me think about how sometimes we get overwhelmed when we would like to do bigger things in the world, and end up not even attempting to start with changes that seem small …

We may not change the whole world –
but we could make a difference.

We shall not wait to feed all the hungry children in Africa, Asia, South America or even Glasgow,

and we shall start here and now
by sharing the food we have with each other.

We shall not wait for border laws to change,
and we shall start now
by opening our homes to strangers and friends.

We shall not wait for the whole world to stop hatred,
discrimination, injustice, oppression,
and we shall start here and now:
through accepting ourselves, our neighbours
and spreading as much kindness as we can.

We shall not wait to serve God in heaven,
and we shall start here and now
through serving those we meet in our daily lives.

Dora Nyamwija, a member of the Resident Group on Iona, from Kenya

Table-setting prayer

As I prepare these places,
may there be a place for Christ
at our table,
in all that is said and shared.

David McNeish

A Psalm from the Abbey Kitchen*

Praise the Lord in the chopping of a carrot.
Praise the Lord in the beating of an egg.
Praise the Lord in the frying of onions.
In all our actions, praise you, Lord.

Praise the Lord in the kneading of bread dough.
Praise the Lord in the baking of a cake.
Praise the Lord in the stirring of porridge.
In all our cooking, praise you, Lord.

Praise the Lord in the washing of dishes.
Praise the Lord in the sweeping of the floor.
Praise the Lord in sanitising surfaces.
Let all our work praise you, Lord.

Praise the Lord in the eating of the food.
Praise the Lord in the drinking of our tea.
Praise the Lord in all our grateful graces.
In all our doing, praise you, Lord!

Jennifer Mayston, a former Iona volunteer

* *The psalm fits the tune of 'Praise the Lord in the playing of the cymbals …' in the* BBC Hymn Book.

Harvest Supper prayer

On this night of warmth amidst the cold,
of light amidst the darkness,
of remembered toil,
worried spring and swollen barley,
we gather gratefully.

We receive from the earth,
and she deserves our generosity in return.
That gifts would be cared for,
and not grasped,
tended and not exploited.

Creating God,
your blessing sings through this food and drink.
May we too sing of your goodness
and delight in your joy,
sharing together in the crop of kindness.
Amen

David McNeish

Prayer for Rogation Sunday

On this Rogation Sunday
we give you thanks for the miracle of growth.
And we pray for those who nurture growing things
so that we can have food and clothing,
and clean air to breathe –
farmers and foresters and fishermen and gardeners.

We pray especially for farmers in the developing world
whose living is always difficult,
and for volunteers with Christian Aid
who sacrifice comfort to give them help.
We give you thanks that you have set us
in a land that is green and plentiful,
rich in its rivers and its seas,
blessed with both rain and sunshine.

Lord of all living things,
help us to sense that human work
in planting and in husbandry
is work alongside you.
Help us to see in every plough
the hand that shaped the ploughs in Nazareth,
and in every growing seed,
help us to see the Kingdom growing patiently
through Jesus Christ, our Lord.

Roddy Cowie

Prayers for when I can't pray

A prayer for when I can't pray (1)

I can't pray today.
Sorry!
I'm in a bad place.
So I'll just leave the book
open at this page
and you can fill in
the words that are missing.

Thanks.
Amen

A prayer for when I can't pray (2)

I can't pray today …
can't get started …
no point.
But if you listen
when I say nothing
you'll hear other people
praying my prayers for me.
I can't pray today –

but they can.
OK?
Amen

A prayer for when I can't pray (3)

I can't pray today …
No reason.
Just nothing to say.
So, can I make a suggestion?
Why not remember the prayers
I offered yesterday
and last week,
and fifteen years ago
when I could pray better
than I can now?
That'll do.
Amen

A prayer for when I can't pray (4)

I can't pray today.
So there it is!
Maybe just saying that
is better than nothing.
Eh?

Well,
it's all you're going to get …
Amen

A prayer for when I can't pray (5)

I can't pray today.
That's the truth.
D'you want the truth?
Are you ready for the truth?
Can you handle the truth?
Life, my God,
is no more or less
than a spectrum of shittiness.
So where am I today?
I'm at the shitty end of shitty.
That's the truth of it.
Got that?
And tomorrow?
If you're still around
I might just give you
the honest truth
about that too.

A prayer for when I can't pray (6)

I can't pray today.
So, tough!
You'll just have to wait.
And you might have to wait
a very long time,
maybe forever –
if you're still around
then …

Tom Gordon

We bring you everything, and tip it out in front of you
(intercessions for an evening service)

Lord God,
we bring to you our happiness and our weariness,
our disappointments and our hopes,
our needs, worldly and spiritual,
our friends and those we find ourselves at odds with,
our families and all the strangers we pass, day in, day out,
and all the billions we will neither know nor pass,
the places that we most love,
and the places that disturb us most profoundly,
our memories and our visions of the future,

our highest successes and our most miserable failures,
the help we offer and the help we need.

We bring you everything,
and tip it out in front of you.

And now we pause a while in silence,
waiting for you to show us what we need to understand …

Lord God, light up the things we need to see,
brush to one side the things we need to put out of our minds,
show us the doors we need to open
and the paths we need to take,
and be beside us as we go
so that the work we do is your work,
and the roads are your roads,
leading to your presence.

We ask it in the name of your son,
and our brother,
Jesus Christ.
Amen

Roddy Cowie

Go well: a meditation for coming times

May the silence speak to you.
May hopefulness lead you.
May forgiveness drive you.
May compassion fill you.
May love compel you:
to overcome hate, whatever the cost,
to welcome the lost and the suffering,
to celebrate difference,
to stand up for justice,
to work for peace,
to believe change is possible,
that good will prevail.

May this coming year
be all you wish it to be:
for yourself,
for those whom you love,
for neighbours and strangers,
for those with whom you disagree,
and for those who choose to see themselves as your enemy.
Go well …

Ewan Aitken

I would have my heart

I would have my heart
be still
the well of you;

I would have my mind
be still
the thought of you;

I would have my voice
be still
except of you;

I would have my work
be still
honest to you;

I would have my home
be still
the joy of you;

I would have my days
be still
the road with you;

I would have my end
be still
alive with you.

Tim Aldred

The Good Shepherd

Lord Jesus, Good Shepherd,
we give you thanks for leading your people
through the dark valleys
to sunlight and green pastures.

We give you thanks for the assurance that each one of us is held
securely in your care
and you will give us joy where there was sorrow,
and laughter where there were tears.

We give you thanks for the joy we feel now
as sunlight returns after the darkness of winter.

We give you thanks
that after the long darkness of conflict
light returns, bit by bit,
and the longing for peace and justice
that you set in human hearts
gradually cracks the ice that gripped us for so long.

We give you thanks for your promise that
in the end
the universe will blossom into the glory that you planned for it
and we will know what it means to be called Children of God.

Almighty God, loving father and Good Shepherd,
we give you thanks for leading us.
We ask you also for the strength, the wisdom and the humility
to follow where you lead.
Through Jesus Christ our Lord
Amen

Roddy Cowie

A repertoire of prayers

I have a repertoire of prayers that I repeat often while I am on the subway or walking. When I'm not travelling in my work for Nonviolent Peaceforce, in places like South Sudan, I spend most of my time in New York City. Walking down the street there, I often say these prayers aloud, which doesn't make me the least bit out of place on the streets of Manhattan, where every other person is either talking to him/herself or on a mobile phone. The prayers include: the Lord's Prayer, the Beatitudes, the Prayer of St Francis (even though he probably didn't write it), some verses from Thich Nhat Hanh, the 7th step prayer from the 12 steps of Alcoholics Anonymous and, the most challenging for me, AA's Acceptance prayer.

About a decade ago, a friend gave me the Acceptance prayer on a laminated card. I stuck it in my wallet and forgot about it. A few months later I was travelling in a dangerous place. I was riding in the back of a vehicle. The journey would take a couple of hours so I pulled out the card and memorised the prayer. This one provokes arguments with God: 'What do you mean the brutal war in South Sudan is exactly how it is meant to be? ... Syria? If that's the best you can do, then F____ off.' During one of my tirades, I heard God say, 'Well, at least we still have a relationship.' I will probably struggle with this prayer for the rest of my days:

> *Acceptance is the answer to all of my problems today. When I am disturbed, it is because I find some person, place, thing or situation – some fact of my life – unacceptable to me, and I can find no serenity until I accept that person, place, thing or situation as being exactly the way it is supposed to be at this moment. Nothing, absolutely nothing, happens in God's world by mistake ...*[1]

Mel Duncan, associate of the Iona Community and co-founder of Nonviolent Peaceforce, www.nonviolentpeaceforce.org

You go before us

You go before us, God of the prophets,
in the green places and in the hard places.
You go before us
with a vision which unsettles us,
with words which transform us.
You look into the heart of life
and turn us away from the shallow
towards the truth.

You go before us, Jesus,
on the long and dusty road to Jerusalem.
You go before us
with courage which inspires us,
with compassion which embraces us.
You look into our hearts
and lead us away from the powers of the world
towards freedom.

You go before us.
You bring us the promise of your kingdom –
with food for the hungry,
healing of the sick,
with freedom from harm,
and peace.

You go before us.
Sometimes we see you.
Sometimes we just miss you.
We want to follow you but we are afraid.
We are afraid of the cost to ourselves.
We hurt you and one another
and we pray for forgiveness …

But then, deep within us,
your word comes to us.
We hear your voice:
'Follow me.'
For where we are, you are.
When we are lost, you are there.
When we are in pieces, you make us whole.

Lord's Prayer …

Susan Miller

With your justice and peace at its heart
(a prayer for the Iona Community)

Lord of our journey,
which begins in the first glimmer that you are there
and that you love me:
thank you for all those I meet on the same journey,
especially for those with me in the Iona Community.

Thank you for our faith,
and our willingness to ask hard questions about faith.
Thank you for our willingness
to share our vulnerability with each other,
and all our difficulties in being a Christian today.

Thank you most of all for our willingness to see you, Jesus,
in all those who feel excluded from society by poverty,
by sexuality, by nationality or any other barrier.
Please strengthen us in our conviction
that we must build a community for everyone,
with your justice and peace at its heart. Amen

Peter Cope, a member of the Iona Community

Sources and acknowledgements

1. p.100: '*Acceptance is the answer to all of my problems today …*' © Alcoholics Anonymous 4th Edition, page 407; reprinted with permission of A.A. World Services, Inc.

About the authors

Ewan Aitken is a former politician and parish minster and is now CEO of Cyrenians, a homelessness charity that supports people excluded from family, home, work or community (http://cyrenians.scot). He has been a member of the Iona Community for 30 years.

Tim Aldred is an associate member of the Iona Community, and is currently Head of Policy and Research at the Fairtrade Foundation (www.fairtrade.org.uk). He lives in Bromley with Sally and their children.

Lisa Bodenheim is an ordained minister in the United Church of Christ in Minnesota. In 2013 her church, Clark-Grace United Church of Christ, part-nered alongside an African-American pastor and his congregation to become one faith community. Lisa is the author of *Disturbing Complacency* (Wild Goose Publications).

Anna Briggs is a member of the Iona Community and a hospital chaplain in Caithness.

Peter Cope spent 40 years as an industrial chaplain in different parts of Britain, and has been an Iona Community member since 1991. Besides assisting his wife, Melia, in Christian ministry in mid-Wales, he greatly enjoys hillwalking, choral singing, playing big band swing, and visiting family around London.

Roddy Cowie is a retired professor who taught psychology at Queen's, Belfast, and helped to pioneer 'affective computing'. He is currently working on projects concerned with self-knowledge and the relationship between Christianity and emotion, as well as writing songs. His web pages are at https://sites.google.com/site/roddycowie/home. He is an Iona associate and a lay reader in the Church of Ireland.

Susan Dale is an Iona Community member and narrative therapist, researcher and writer living in Devon.

Kerry Davies is an associate member of the Iona Community who lives in Hessle, near Hull, Yorkshire, with his wife Ros and their four children. He is a freelance artist and illustrator who has worked on various Iona projects, including illustrations for Wild Goose Publications. You can view his artwork at www.facebook.com/KdArtUk

Mel Duncan is a co-founder and current Director of Advocacy and Outreach for Nonviolent Peaceforce (NP), a world leader in unarmed civilian protection (www.nonviolentpeaceforce.org). NP provides direct protection to civilians caught in violent conflict and works with local groups on violence deterrence in a variety of conflict areas around the world. Mel represents NP at the United Nations, where the group has been granted consultative status. The Presbyterian Peace Fellowship honoured Mel with their 2010 Peace Seeker award. The Fellowship of Reconciliation USA awarded him their 2007 Pfeffer International Peace Prize, on behalf of Nonviolent Peaceforce's *'courageous efforts in conflict regions around the world'*. *Utne Reader* named him as one of '50 visionaries who are changing our world'. The American Friends Service Committee nominated Nonviolent Peaceforce for the 2016 Nobel Peace Prize. Mel and his wife, Georgia, associates of the Community, have 8 children and 12 grandchildren. Mel is a legendary Abbey guide.

Emily D'Silva was a volunteer housekeeper at the Abbey in the summer of 2016, and is now part of the Resident staff team.

Liz England: 'I am an ordained Priest in the Church of England and currently serve full-time in the Parish of Codsall in Staffordshire. I am married, with two sons, and enjoy dancing, painting and cinema.'

Andrew Foster: An engineer, an elder in the Presbyterian Church in Canada, a frequent visitor to Iona and a contributor to a number of Wild Goose books.

Ewen Gilchrist has been a Kirk minister in three very different parishes, and slowly realised that praying was an opportunity to be painfully, wonderfully and sometimes comically honest in the presence of God.

Elaine Gisbourne is a member of the Iona Community, living in Lancaster, where she works as a palliative care physiotherapist and a spiritual director. Elaine has contributed to a number of Wild Goose Publications.

Tom Gordon is a retired Church of Scotland minister and former Marie Curie hospice chaplain. He currently gives his time to writing, teaching and facilitating bereavement support groups. He is the author of several books (Wild Goose Publications), and his writing embraces contemporary parables, daily reflections, bereavement issues, liturgy, social concerns and poetry. He has been a member of the Iona Community since 1973 and lives with his wife, Mary, in East Lothian.

John Harvey is a member of the Iona Community and a retired Church of Scotland minister. He served as Warden of Iona Abbey and as Leader of the Iona Community, and in the 1980s was the minister of Govan Old Parish Church in Glasgow.

Frances Hawkey: 'Having been privileged to live in a wide variety of communities in different places and situations – rural Kent, Bombay, Berkshire, an inner-city London council estate, centres of reconciliation in Iona and Coventry … – I have learnt to be mindful and thankful for all I have received. It has also made me conscious of those for whom life is *not* easy. I try to balance these two aspects in my prayers and actions.'

Susan Lindsay: 'I lived on Iona and worked as a volunteer cook in the MacLeod Centre, before becoming Head Housekeeper of the Abbey for two seasons. I now live in Burntisland with my cat Henry and work as Head Gardener at Aberdour Castle. I am a new member of the Iona Community, and based my new members project around the issue of occupation in the West Bank. This included a trip to Bethlehem, Jerusalem and Hebron. I continue to be passionate about Israel/Palestine and peace and justice.'

Peter Lloyd, and Liz Lloyd, with their golden lab, Rory, returned to Scotland in October 2016. During their eight years abroad they had been active supporting migrants through their leadership of the project 'Out of Africa into Malta'. They have settled into their new home in Perth and remain committed to the support of refugees.

Jennifer Mayston: 'I first went to Iona, staying in the youth camps, in 1962, then returned several times as a volunteer from 2008, when I also became an associate member of the Community.'

Rachel McCann is a gardener, activist, cook, writer and member of the Iona Community.

David McNeish lives and works in the West Mainland of Orkney with his family, dog and guitars. He is the minister of Milestone Community Church, and chair of Orkney Pilgrimage, the group behind the establishment of the St Magnus Way, a 55-mile pilgrimage route inspired by the life and journeys of Magnus: www.stmagnusway.com

Peter Millar is a former warden of Iona Abbey, who has worked in India, Glasgow, Africa and Australia. He is the author of several books, including *An Iona Prayer Book* (Canterbury Press), *Finding Hope Again* (Canterbury

Press), *A Time to Mend* (Wild Goose Publications) and *Our Hearts Still Sing* (Wild Goose). He is a soul friend to many.

Susan Miller is a locum minister in the Church of Scotland at Ibrox Parish Church. She also teaches courses in New Testament at Glasgow University, and has published *Women in Mark's Gospel* (Continuum, 2004).

Israel Nelson is an associate member of the Iona Community in Alaska. He is an ordained Minister of Word and Sacrament, or Teaching Elder, in the Presbyterian Church (USA) and is now retired. He 'came into the country' of Alaska in 1998 and served first in McGrath as Executive Director of 4Rivers Counselling Services, treating mental health and substance abuse issues. In 2000 he moved to Palmer and the Matanuska-Susitna Valley, where he serves as Assessment Counsellor for Alaska Family Services. With exposure to Alaska native peoples he has developed a deep appreciation for their mystical spirituality. He is a volunteer Board of Directors member for Habitat for Humanity Mat-Su and for Family Promise Mat-Su, an emergency shelter programme for children and their parents.

Dora Nyamwija became aware of the injustices and difficulties faced by people with disabilities while growing up in Uganda in a school for special needs children, which her father helped to run. While working on Iona, she was inspired to raise awareness and money to help change the lives of special needs children in Uganda, by fundraising to provide accessible toilets. She started with the school she had grown up in and, through many folk's generosity, has now raised nearly enough money for accessible toilets in four schools. Dora plans to return to Uganda, after four years as a housekeeper at the MacLeod Centre, to marry her patient boyfriend, Tom, and to continue her work for change: www.gofundme.com/accessloosuganda.

David Osborne has worked as an engineer in Edinburgh, a teacher in Somerset and Nigeria, and a vicar in Shropshire and Somerset. He is now retired and works voluntarily with Christian Aid. He is the author of several books, including *Love for the Future: A Journey* (Wild Goose Publications), which recommends forms of spirituality for responding to the ecological crisis. He is a member of the Iona Community.

Neil Paynter is an editor, writer and late-night piano player, who lives with his partner Helen, his mum and Stevie the cat in a flat in Biggar, Scotland. Previously he worked in homeless shelters in Canada and the UK.

Jan Sutch Pickard is a poet, preacher and storyteller living in Mull. She worked in the Iona Community's centres on Iona for six years, and served with EAPPI in the West Bank. She is the author of *A Pocket Full of Crumbs* and other books and downloads (Wild Goose Publications).

Chris Polhill is a member of the Iona Community and one of the first women priests in the Church of England. She has contributed to a number of Wild Goose books and is the author of *Eggs and Ashes* (with Ruth Burgess), *A Pilgrim's Guide to Iona Abbey*, *A Heart for Creation* and *In the Mists on the Shoreline* (Wild Goose). She and her husband, John, run the Reflection Gardens, which highlights the Christian spiritual journey and environmental issues.

Rosemary Power is a member of the Iona Community and currently its Prayer Circle Coordinator. She works in church ministry and also as a writer and speaker, specialising in new forms of ministry, social justice and the arts. She works academically as a historian and folklorist. She is the author of *The Story of Iona* (Canterbury Press).

Richard Sharples is a Methodist minister in Bristol, where he is seeking to use the arts as a means of mission, and to cycle as much as possible. He is married to Biddy, and both are members of the Iona Community.

Thom M Shuman is a retired minister, currently engaged in transitional ministry. He is passionate about the most vulnerable in our midst, especially persons with mental illness. He is an associate member of the Iona Community, and the author of books and downloads, including *The Soft Petals of Grace* (Wild Goose Publications). He continues to practise the spiritual discipline of writing daily.

Isabel Whyte: 'I grew up in the West of Scotland and first visited Iona as a youth camper in 1961. I became a Youth associate and was involved in the camps as a camper, a cook and a camp leader. My husband Iain and I met leading an Iona camp in 1965. We married in 1967. I have been a teacher and hospital chaplain and always involved in peacemaking and justice and peace issues – most recently picking olives in Palestine and in conflict transformation as part of Place for Hope.'